Redford Township District Library
25320 West Six Mile Road
Redford, MI 48240

www.redford.lib.mi.us

Hours:

Mon–Thur 10–8:30
Fri–Sat 10–5
Sunday (School Year) 12–5

Illustrated History of
MARTIAL ARTS

NINJA

by Jerry Craven

illustrated by Jean Dixon

THE ROURKE CORPORATION, INC.
VERO BEACH, FL 32964

ACKNOWLEDGMENTS

I am grateful to Jean Dixon both for her wonderful art and for the care she took researching Japanese artwork in order to make sure her paintings are genuine reflections of Japanese culture. Also, I thank Samio and Lauri Watanabe for helping me understand the tourist industry based on ninja history in the city of Iga-Ueno.

PHOTO CREDITS

Lauri Watanabe: page 6.
All other photos courtesy of Ueno Sightseeing Association, Iga-Ueno, Japan.

© 1994 The Rourke Corporation, Inc.

Library of Congress Cataloging-in-Publication Data

Craven, Jerry
    Ninja / by Jerry Craven.
      p. cm. — (Illustrated history of martial arts)
    Includes index.
    ISBN 0-86593-365-0
    1. Ninjutsu—Juvenile literature. [1. Ninjutsu.] I. Title. II. Series.
UB271.J3C73 1994
355.5'48—dc20   94-2528
                                                          CIP

Printed in the USA   AC

TABLE OF CONTENTS

Hundreds of years ago in Japan, people feared and hated the ninja, for they were tricksters trained to kill. The ninja practiced the art of *ninjutsu,* using disguises and lies, special skills with weaponry – and often striking down their victims in the dark.

There were ninja as early as the 16th century. However, some historians say the *idea* of the ninja dates back to ancient China, to the writing of Sun Tzu. The oldest book on warfare is *The Art of War,* written by Sun Tzu over 2,500 years ago. Sun Tzu recommended that generals attack an enemy only after sending in agents to disrupt normal life. The agents were to work in disguise or under the cover of darkness, creating discord by assassinating important leaders.

A Japanese ambassador to China brought the ideas of Sun Tzu to Japan sometime in the eighth century. Perhaps the Japanese ninja date from that period. The story of Prince Yamato, sometimes called an early ninja, comes from that time.

Sent to the southern Japanese island of Kyushu to put down a rebellion, Yamato disguised himself as a young woman. He was so beautiful that the two rebel chieftains invited him to sit between them at a banquet. Yamato took a sword from under his dress and killed the chieftains.

The disguise, the hidden sword and the assassination later became parts of the ninja tradition.

An early ninja, Prince Yamato disguised himself as a woman so he could get close to some rebel chieftains. He took a samurai sword from under his dress and assassinated the rebels.

2

THE FIRST NINJA

ASSASSIN

Kumawaka was only 13 years old when he became the first ninja assassin.

His victim was Homma Saburo, a man who had killed Kumawaka's father. While a guest in Saburo's home, Kumawaka pretended to be ill during the day so he could sneak around the house and plan his crime. He discovered where Saburo slept.

On the night of the crime, Saburo had changed bedrooms, but Kumawaka found him. Since he had no sword, Kumawaka decided to use Saburo's weapon. However, he feared the lamp burning in the bedroom might throw his shadow in a way that would awaken Saburo.

In a ninja home now made into a museum, this tour guide shows how ancient ninja assassins hid their weapons. The ninja museum is in the Japanese city Iga-Ueno.

Kumawaka, the first ninja, escaped after his crime by lowering himself on bamboo across a moat.

Kumawaka put out the lamp with clever trick. He noticed a swarm of moths by the door, trying to get to the light. So he opened the door and watched as the moths swarmed around the lamp, extinguishing it.

With his victim's own sword, Kumawaka killed Saburo. The assassin then fled to a bamboo thicket behind the house. When he heard the sounds of the house guards in pursuit, Kumawaka escaped across a moat with another clever trick. He climbed a bamboo until his weight bent the plant, lowering him across the moat.

Kumawaka committed his crime hundreds of years ago, before there were ninja. However, because he used the kind of trickery that later ninja assassins became famous for, many consider him the first ninja.

3

SAMURAI

AND NINJA

For the samurai warrior, the proper weapon was the sword, and the proper way to fight was in the open, in the full light of day. Samurai valued loyalty and skill in fighting so much that these warriors often praised an enemy who fought well. It was important to the samurai to win at war. It was equally important to win in an honorable way.

Samurai valued a frontal attack. It was a high honor to be the first into battle. It was natural, then, that the samurai would hate the ninja. The word "ninja" comes from two Japanese words that mean "a person who hides." Samurai scorned the use of disguises, so common among ninja.

Even worse was the ninja habit of sneaking into castles to attack with a knife in the dark. A general might hire ninja to help take a castle – and the samurai might be in awe of the ability of the ninja to scale a wall or sneak into a fort – but the warriors hated ninja for not fighting in the open.

During the 16th century, rival warlords often hired ninja as soldiers. Unlike the samurai who served from loyalty, the ninja fought for pay. There were times when one family of ninja sold their services to different armies who were at war with each other.

Just as this ninja was about to kill his victim, a samurai palace guard caught him from behind.

Actors pose for tourists at the Ueno Castle in Iga-Ueno, Japan. These colorful costumes are not authentic. Ninja almost always wore black.

In the 1570s, when Japanese warlords, or *daimyo*, fought one another for control of territory, many daimyo hired ninja to kill rivals.

A wise daimyo surrounded himself with troops, even in his home. An extreme case, Takeda Shingen, had 6,373 bodyguards.

Even with many household troops, daimyos felt unsafe sleeping without a club or a dagger close at hand. The most dangerous time for a daimyo was when he was recovering from battle wounds. Most leaders kept several "safe houses" hidden in the mountains, where they could go to recover from wounds without worrying about ninja assassins.

The daimyo used other tricks to foil the feared ninja. Some kept rice paper on the floor of their bedrooms so guards would be alerted if anyone walked on it. Others installed special bedroom floors that creaked.

The Nijo Castle in the city of Kyoto, built in 1600, is an example of an attempt to make a whole building ninja-proof. "Nightingale floors" are all over the castle. They are made from wood and balanced to make loud squeaks, like the singing of nightingales, if anyone walks upon them.

The precautions of the daimyo show how much they feared the nighttime trickery of the deadly ninja assassins.

These ninja warriors have captured the lord of a castle and are trying to get military secrets from him.

5

THE NINJA

SUPERMAN

Ninja learned to fight with the weapons of the samurai. Ninja also learned to use other weapons as well as tricks such as crossing moats, climbing walls, walking without making noise, and sneaking past guards at night. Many people were so awed by the skills of the ninja that they believed the ninja used magic.

Some said ninja could fly, others said that ninja could walk on water. Some even claimed that a ninja could come back from the dead.

Ninja liked the reputation of being supermen. It made people afraid, and fear was a useful weapon. One famous ninja, Kakei Juzo, wanted people to think he was dead and his ghost was continuing his ninja work.

Kakei Juzo made it look as if he committed *seppuku*, or suicide, in a public place. People saw him push his sword into his stomach, then collapse in a bloody heap. His body was thrown into a moat.

Kakei Juzo swam from the moat and escaped. The blood people saw came from a dead fox that he had under his robe. His trick worked. When he returned to practice his ninja arts, those who saw him were terrified because they thought they were seeing a ghost.

One famous ninja, Ishikawa Goemon, claimed to be able to summon spirits by using magic signs with his fingers.

12

6

DEADLY NINJA

S K I L L S

Ninja of the 16th century guarded their secret knowledge. They took care to pass knowledge of martial arts only from father to son, or from master to student. Ninja killed anyone caught teaching their skills to the wrong people.

Some ninja masters wrote secret training manuals. In later years, during times of peace when there was no need of ninja, the manuals were published.

One skill useful to the nighttime assassin was seeing in the dark. Ninja learned special ways to see with little light. They worked at keeping their pupils dilated by never looking directly at a lamp or even a candle.

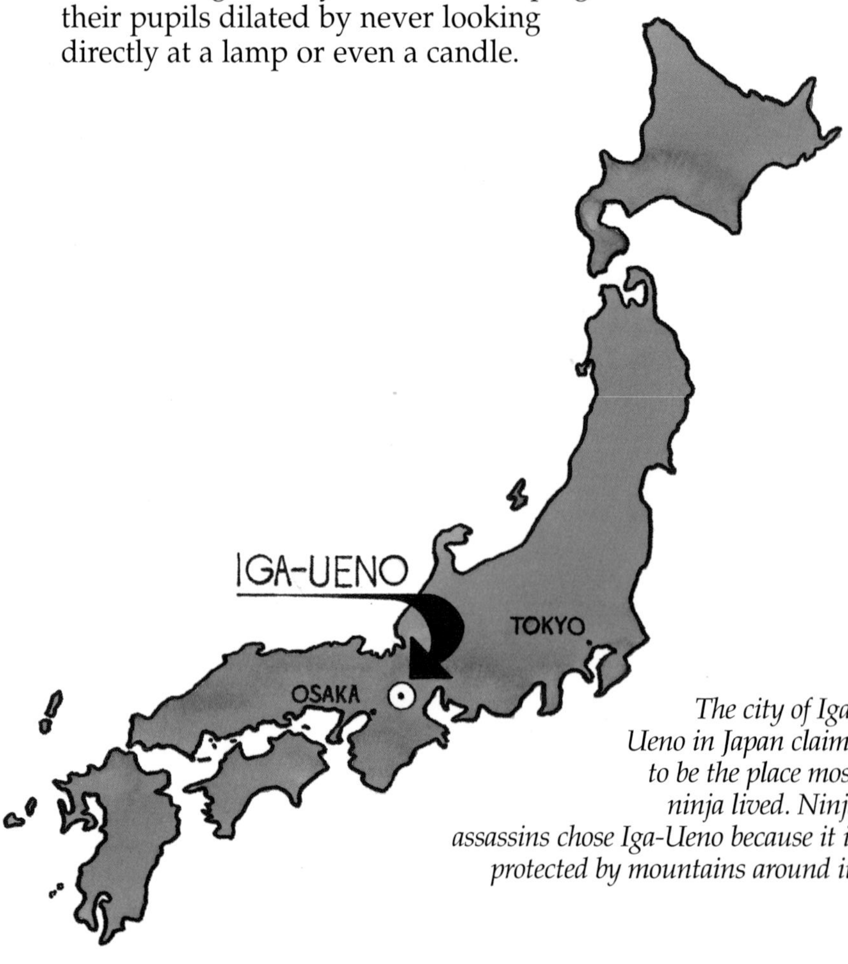

IGA-UENO

TOKYO

OSAKA

The city of Iga-Ueno in Japan claims to be the place most ninja lived. Ninja assassins chose Iga-Ueno because it is protected by mountains around it.

An important skill of the ninja was the ability to sneak into castles.

Another skill was to analyze snoring. A good assassin needed to know how sound asleep his victims and guards might be. Ninja studied snoring patterns of both men and women, in order to know who was faking sleep. One ninja guideline was to first kill anyone pretending to be asleep, then to kill the intended victim.

An important survival skill for ninja was hiding through disguise. A ninja had to learn to pass as an ordinary person during the day. Among the disguises recommended by ninja manuals were a dancer, a flute-player, a merchant, a priest and a *yamabushi* (a mountain pilgrim). The clothing of all of these people was good for both disguise and for hiding weapons.

7

NINJA

M
E
D
I
C
I
N
E

A ninja used medicines made from plants to cure himself of sickness and to poison victims.

Most ninja carried a medicine called moxa. Moxa is scraped from the underside of mugwort leaves. It is a yellow substance that catches fire easily. The ninja would place a cone of it somewhere on his skin, then set the moxa on fire. The ninja knew about 360 spots on the body where burning moxa was supposed to be a cure. Each spot was supposed to relate to an internal organ. The ninja would decide which organ was causing his illness, then select the place for burning the moxa.

Poison was also a ninja tool. One way ninja assassins delivered poison was by hiding in a ceiling at night and lowering a thread to the mouth of a sleeping victim. The ninja would dribble poison down the thread into the mouth of the person he wanted to kill.

Tobi Kato, a ninja people believed knew magic, used poison for his tricks. To test Tobi Kato's skills, a warlord challenged the ninja to steal a weapon in a house guarded by a large dog. Tobi Kato killed the dog by feeding it poisoned rice, then entered the house and stole the weapon. He also carried out an 11-year-old servant girl, just to show how sneaky he could be.

Ninja were skilled at getting in and out of castles undetected. They knew if they got caught by guards, they would be facing samurai skilled in such martial arts as jujitsu.

THE MAGIC NINJA

Many people in ancient Japan believed that a ninja could fly across castle moats. Some claimed a ninja could become invisible and even walk on ceilings. The "magic" powers of ninja were respected and feared for several reasons. First, the Japanese had a traditional belief in magic. In addition, the great skills of the ninja must have seemed magical to the nontrained.

Many believed the ninja came from the yamabushi, a religious group whose members were supposed to be able to speak with animals and control fire with their minds. The word "yamabushi" means "the ones who lie down on mountains." It refers to men who believed they could gain special powers from mountain pilgrimages, and from exercises such as meditating to overcome discomfort while sitting in a waterfall.

Some legends tell of yamabushi trained by mountain goblins called *tengu*, who were part crow and part man. Tengu were supposed to be experts with swords and to know magic.

The tengu, according to legend, taught ninja how to change into a rat or a spider to do the work of an assassin, and how to change into a bird to escape. Such legends show the fear people had of ninja. It wasn't until modern times that people began to admire the ninja.

Tengu, trickster goblins who were half men and half crow, supposedly taught some ninja how to fight with swords.

FAMOUS NINJA

Fuma Kotaro was good at taking small groups of ninja into an enemy camp. In 1581, he led a series of raids against the troops of Takeda Katsuyori. Each night, the ninja would sneak away with swords, armor and other loot from the Takeda camp.

When the samurai of Takeda Katsuyori tried to get close to the raiding ninja to attack them, Fuma Kotaro's men stopped the attack with a ninja trick. The samurai mingled among the raiders, passing themselves off as ninja. However, on a secret signal, the ninja stooped down, exposing those among them who were not ninja. The trick identified their enemy and saved the ninja from ambush.

Another famous ninja, Saiga Magoichi, won a major battle by leading his ninja under the flag of the enemy. This made the enemy think the ninja were allies. The trick allowed ninja soldiers to get close enough for a surprise attack.

Samurai considered Saiga Magoichi's trick with flags to be dishonorable. The ninja, however, believed any trick was fair – so long as it brought victory.

Ishikawa Goemon was a criminal who was elevated to the status of ninja hero by folk tales. In real life, he was hardly heroic. At age 16, he robbed his master, then killed the men sent to arrest him. His life of crime ended in 1595 when he was caught and executed by being boiled in oil.

This is Ishikawa Goemon, one of the famous ninja in Japanese folklore. In real life, Goemon was a criminal.

This ninja is wearing body armor designed to look like
a tengu, the mythological goblin that was half crow and half man.

THE DEADLY

SHURIKEN

When guards chased a ninja assassin, the ninja sometimes paused to throw what is now known as "ninja stars." These were a variety of *shuriken*, or hand-thrown weapons. The ninja had a number of kinds of shuriken.

Ninja stars are flat disks made from hammered iron or steel. They have several sharpened points designed to cut into the flesh of pursuing guards. They were seldom fatal because they were so small and inaccurate. Guards wore armor that stopped the shuriken, so the ninja aimed for the few unarmored areas of the body: hands, face and neck.

Shuriken also included darts that look like large nails, and knives designed for throwing. Some ninja no doubt coated the blades of the stars and the tips of the darts with poison. Few poisons, though, kill immediately. A ninja didn't use the shuriken to kill. He used them to slow down pursuers and to cause guards to be afraid.

Poison was hardly necessary. A cut from a dirty blade could cause a bad enough infection to inflict great pain and sometimes even death. Guards who had seen the long-term results of a shuriken wound no doubt disliked getting close to a fleeing ninja.

The ninja valued fear as a weapon, and the shuriken was good at causing fear.

This is a scene from a play acted for tourists in the Japanese city Iga-Ueno, famous for being the home of ninja in past centuries.

11

UNUSUAL NINJA

E Q U I P M E N T

Ninja had several devices for crossing water. The least useful were "watershoes." These were blocks of wood a ninja attached to his feet. Similar devices were two large pots that fit over the feet and were supposed to allow ninja to walk across water. A better device for crossing moats was a *shinobi-fune,* a small collapsible boat. This device could be folded down into a box one person could carry.

The only large device actually used by ninja was something that could pass for an armored tank. It was a battering ram on a cart that had a protective roof and walls, and was used against the Koreans in the late 16th century.

Less unusual and more useful to the stealth assassin were caltrops. Called *tetsu-bishi,* these were small metal spikes. A ninja could drop these when being chased. They always land with one spike straight up, and were effective because Japanese in the 16th century wore straw-bottomed sandals.

Like most people in the 16th century, ninja were superstitious. Before going on a mission, many ninja prepared a charm to ensure success. Using his own blood as ink, the ninja would write some lucky words or signs on a piece of paper. He would carry the blood charm close to his body.

Ninja wore black cloth cowls or hats and facial masks. Because ninja assassins wanted to keep their identity secret, it would make them angry to have their face masks removed.

12

A NINJA'S

K N A P S A C K

What a ninja carried with him depended on the job he was hired to do and how long it was going to take. In addition to small weapons, a ninja carried a number of items to help him survive an assignment.

Because ninja often had to crawl through grass, snakes were a danger. Snake-bite medicine was a normal item in most ninja knapsacks.

If a ninja became thirsty or hungry, he might take a thirst pill or a hunger pill from his knapsack. Ninja made thirst pills by using a stone to grind up four parts of pickled plums, one part of rock candy, and one part of winter wheat. Then they rolled the mixture into pills.

Ingredients for Ninja Thirst Pills

$\frac{1}{2}$ ounce of pickled plums
$\frac{1}{4}$ tablespoon of winter wheat
$\frac{1}{4}$ tablespoon of rock candy

This actress is hiding a scroll of information under the floor of a ninja house. The color of the costume isn't authentic, but it makes for interesting drama. Most ninja were men, though there were a few women who trained and worked as ninja.

In the 19th century, one ninja trick was to lie on the battlefield, pretending to be dead, and then shoot enemy soldiers who came near. Ninja who did this were called "human bombs."

Making hunger pills was a bit more complicated. The ingredients were simple enough:

10	ounces each of buckwheat flour, wheat flour, mountain potato, and glutinous rice
5	ounces each of ginseng and yokui kernels
½	ounce of chickweed
5	ounces of ginseng
3	pints of saké

The time-consuming part was the preparation. The ninja mixed the dry ingredients, then soaked them in *saké,* or rice wine, until the wine was absorbed and the mixture had dried to a starchy goo. The ninja rolled the goo into balls the size of a peach. One batch made enough hunger pills to last for one day.

A ninja had to keep his knapsack light, so he restricted its contents to only essential items.

13

AMUSING NINJA

S K I L L S

Some ancient ninja skills strike people today as humorous. Among these were:

✳ **Using a Cat Clock.** Three hundred years ago, ninja believed they could tell time by looking at the eyes of a cat. At six in the morning, a cat's eyes were supposed to be half open and the pupils round. At nine, the eyes would be almost fully open, and the pupils were narrowed to fine points at the bottom. At noon, the cat's eyes were supposed to be fully open and the pupils reduced to thin vertical lines.

✳ **Wearing Extra Heads.** In battle, ninja used tricks to confuse the enemy. One was to wear a fake head on each shoulder.

The idea was that a three-headed soldier would unnerve the enemy, perhaps causing panic in the ranks. Those brave enough to face a three-headed man had a problem. Which way do you face someone with three faces, each turned a different direction?

✳ **Walking on Paper.** Because of the danger of nighttime ninja attacks, warlords, or daimyos, placed crinkly rice paper on bedroom floors. Anyone walking on the brittle floor covering would awaken the daimyo or alert nearby bodyguards. Ninja overcame the problem by learning special techniques for walking on rice paper without making noise.

Among the more unusual skills of ninja was their supposed ability to tell time by looking at the eyes of a cat.

猫の眼時計

14

NINJA TODAY

Those today who practice ninjutsu, or the art of the ninja, are redefining what a ninja is. In the past, the ninja sold his skills at warfare, assassination and spying.

However, today many people admire the ninja of the past for their martial arts skills. Modern teachers of ninja skills often claim that the history of the ninja as hired killers is inaccurate. Such a claim, however, does not match the facts of history.

Today, some people are developing a new tradition of the ninja. Those who study ninja skills regard them as a martial art for self-protection and as a fun hobby. They see modern ninjutsu as a way to live a moral life.

Teachers such as Dr. Masaaki Hastsumi in Japan and Stephen K. Hayes in the United States are helping redefine ninjutsu in good ways. Both teach ninjutsu as an art of self-defense, and they condemn the violence of criminals.

These are school children marching in the parade that is part of a festival in Iga-Ueno every March 23-25. The city of Iga-Ueno makes its historical ties with ninja into a tourist industry.

caltrops: metal spikes scattered by escaping ninja; ninja called them tetsu-bishi.

daimyo: Japanese warlords or chieftains during the time of the samurai.

Iga-Ueno: the mountain city in Japan where many ninja lived.

martial arts: any form of military training; often the term refers to empty-handed fighting, as well as to the various forms of exercises and sports developed from ancient fighting skills.

moxa: a flammable material used by ninja to cure various illnesses.

mugwort: a smelly, bitter herb often used in folk medicine. Ninja used it as a source for moxa.

nightingale floors: wooden floors in castles made to squeak if someone walked on them. The squeaking would warn people in the castle if a ninja assassin came in at night.

saké: rice wine.

samurai: a class of elite Japanese warriors who, for hundreds of years, fought the battles of the emperors and warlords.

seppuku: ritual suicide performed by plunging a knife into the lower abdomen.

shinobi-fune: a portable boat that ninja used to get across moats.

shuriken: any of a number of small, sharp objects thrown by ninja when making a getaway. These include ninja stars.

tengu: goblins in Japanese folklore; they were half men and half crow, and they liked to play tricks on people.

tetsu-bishi: caltrops or metal spikes used by ninja to slow down pursuers.

yamabushi: a religious pilgrim who traveled in the mountains of Japan. Sometimes ninja disguised themselves as yamabushi.

GLOSSARY

INDEX